THE SOLAR SYSTEM

SATURN

A MyReportLinks.com Book

STEPHEN FEINSTEIN

MyReportLinks.com Books

an imprint of

Enslow Publishers, Inc.

Box 398, 40 Industrial Road

Berkeley Heights, NJ 07922

MyReportLinks.com Books, an imprint of Enslow Publishers, Inc. MyReportLinks®
is a registered trademark of Enslow Publishers, Inc.

Library of Congress Cataloging-in-Publication Data

Feinstein, Stephen.
  Saturn / Stephen Feinstein.
    p. cm. — (The solar system)
  Includes bibliographical references and index.
  ISBN 0-7660-5304-0
  1. Saturn (Planet)—Juvenile literature. I. Title. II. Solar system (Berkeley Heights, N.J.)
  QB671.F34 2005
  523.46—dc22
                                        2004022957

Printed in the United States of America

10 9 8 7 6 5 4 3 2 1

To Our Readers:
Through the purchase of this book, you and your library gain access to the Report Links that specifically back up this book.
The Publisher will provide access to the Report Links that back up this book and will keep these Report Links up to date on **www.myreportlinks.com** for five years from the book's first publication date.
We have done our best to make sure all Internet addresses in this book were active and appropriate when we went to press. However, the author and the Publisher have no control over, and assume no liability for, the material available on those Internet sites or on other Web sites they may link to.
The usage of the MyReportLinks.com Books Web site is subject to the terms and conditions stated on the Usage Policy Statement on **www.myreportlinks.com**.
A password may be required to access the Report Links that back up this book. The password is found on the bottom of page 4 of this book.
Any comments or suggestions can be sent by e-mail to comments@myreportlinks.com or to the address on the back cover.

Photo Credits: © Nicolaus Copernicus Museum, p. 13; © Windows to the Universe, p. 12; ESA/NASA, pp. 29, 41, 43; European Space Agency (ESA), pp. 15, 16; Lunar and Planetary Institute, p. 10; MyReportLinks.com Books, p. 4; NASA/David Seal, p. 33; NASA/ESA/University of Arizona, p. 31; NASA/JPL/GSFC/Ames, p. 23; NASA/JPL/Johns Hopkins University, p. 18; NASA/JPL/Space Science Institute, pp. 17, 34, 35, 37; NASA/JPL/University of Colorado, p. 25; National Aeronautics and Space Administration (NASA), pp. 1, 3, 9, 20, 21, 27, 39; Photos.com, pp. 3, 9.

Note: Some NASA photos were only available in a low-resolution format.

Cover Photo: National Aeronautics and Space Administration.

About MyReportLinks.com Books

MyReportLinks.com Books
Great Books, Great Links, Great for Research!

The Internet sites listed on the next four pages can save you hours of research time. These Internet sites—we call them "Report Links"—are constantly changing, but we keep them up to date on our Web site.

Give it a try! Type http://www.myreportlinks.com into your browser, click on the series title, then the book title, and scroll down to the Report Links listed for this book.

The Report Links will bring you to great source documents, photographs, and illustrations. MyReportLinks.com Books save you time, feature Report Links that are kept up to date, and make report writing easier than ever!

Please see "To Our Readers" on the copyright page for important information about this book, the MyReportLinks.com Web site, and the Report Links that back up this book.

Please enter **PSA1700** if asked for a password.

Report Links

→ The Internet sites described below can be accessed at
http://www.myreportlinks.com

*EDITOR'S CHOICE

►Saturn: Your Travel Guide to the Solar System
This BBC Web site offers all kinds of information on Saturn. A time
line of exploratory missions to Saturn and interesting facts on what
you would encounter if you were to visit this planet are included.

*EDITOR'S CHOICE

►*Cassini-Huygens*: Mission to Saturn & Titan
The *Cassini-Huygens* mission to Saturn is an international project
involving three space agencies. Beginning in 2004, the spacecraft started
to explore the Saturnian system. Learn about this pioneering space
project at this Web site.

*EDITOR'S CHOICE

►Nineplanets.org: Saturn
Learn all about Saturn and its rings from this Web site. Information on
space probes to the planet and its satellites is also included.

*EDITOR'S CHOICE

►The Galileo Project: Saturn
Galileo was born in Pisa, Italy, on February 15, 1564. He was a
mathematician, an inventor, and an astronomer. This site explains
what happened when he first observed Saturn through his telescope.

*EDITOR'S CHOICE

►Welcome to the Planets: Saturn
Take an online photographic tour of Saturn at this NASA site. View the
planet's rings, moons, and clouds, as well as the crater that William Herschel
discovered on Mimas, one of Saturn's large moons.

*EDITOR'S CHOICE

►Discoverer of Titan: Christiaan Huygens
The Dutch astronomer and mathematician Christiaan Huygens was the
first person to realize that the objects around Saturn were rings. He also
discovered the planet's most important moon, Titan. Read more about
Huygens on this European Space Agency site.

Report Links

The Internet sites described below can be accessed at http://www.myreportlinks.com

▶ Aristarchus Who? of Where?

Aristarchus of Samos was one of the first astronomers to propose that the Sun was the center of the universe. Read more about him on this site from the Ontario Science Centre.

▶ At the Edge of an Alien World: *Cassini* Arrives at Saturn

Learn about the early successes of the *Cassini-Huygens* mission to Saturn. Scientists are already learning a lot more about the planet and its moons and rings since the mission began.

▶ ESA Kids

These Web pages from the European Space Agency (ESA), a partner with NASA on the *Cassini-Huygens* mission to Saturn and Titan, are designed especially for kids and offer information not only on Saturn but also on the rest of the solar system.

▶ European Space Agency: *Cassini-Huygens*

This official *Cassini-Huygens* mission Web site from the European Space Agency contains information on the mission, Saturn, and the planet's moons. View the latest images, and see an animation of where the spacecraft is at any given moment and where it is headed.

▶ Exploring the Planets: Saturn

Take an online tour of Saturn on this site. Text and images are combined to help you learn about the planet and its famous ring system.

▶ Giovanni Domenico Cassini

In 1675, Giovanni Domenico Cassini discovered a gap in Saturn's rings as well as four previously unknown moons. Read a biography of this seventeenth-century astronomer at this Web site.

▶ Hubble Gets Superb View of Saturn and Rings

The Hubble Space Telescope captured detailed photographs of Saturn's southern hemisphere and the southern face and underside of its rings. View these images at this Web site.

▶ Life Beyond Earth: Titan

This PBS site provides the reader with information on Titan, Saturn's largest satellite. Its discovery, size, atmosphere, orbit, and exploratory missions are all discussed here.

Any comments? Contact us: **comments@myreportlinks.com**

Report Links

The Internet sites described below can be accessed at http://www.myreportlinks.com

National Maritime Museum: Saturn

Saturn is one of the most beautiful planets in the solar system with its rings, bands, and numerous moons. This site provides information on Saturn's atmosphere, its larger satellites, and the *Cassini–Huygens* probe.

Nicolaus Copernicus Museum

This Nicolaus Copernicus Museum Web site includes a biography and images of the sixteenth-century Polish astronomer who revolutionized our understanding of the solar system.

NSSDC Photo Gallery: Saturn

NASA has provided a photographic gallery of Saturn images on this site. Take a look at the pictures, and read the captions to learn more about this fascinating planet.

An Observing Guide to Saturn

This Web site offers amateur astronomers a guide to observing Saturn, its rings, and its moons. Information on what to look for and an interactive sky chart is included for best results.

Planetary Photojournal

A large collection of Saturnian images is available on this NASA site. Just follow the links for the planet and its moons. Photographs are accompanied by explanatory text.

The Planets: Saturn

Saturn's atmosphere has three distinct parts or layers, made of clouds. This BBC weather site examines the atmosphere and takes a look at the winds and storms on the ringed planet.

Saturn

This comprehensive site on Saturn from NASA offers a great deal of information on the sixth planet from the Sun as well as images. Included are resources on space missions, fact sheets, and an online book about the Voyager missions.

Saturn: Sixth Planet From the Sun

This Planetary Society Web site on Saturn is a good place to learn about the planet. News, facts, interviews, images, and articles are provided.

Report Links

The Internet sites described below can be accessed at http://www.myreportlinks.com

▶**Saturn's Atmosphere**

Composed primarily of hydrogen and helium, Saturn is a very cold and windy planet that has violent storms. This article is only a small part of the larger European Space Agency Web site for Saturn.

▶**Saturn's Ring System**

The particles in Saturn's rings are made primarily of ice, rock, and dirt. This NASA site provides information on and images of the ring system and includes a movie of the mysterious spokes in Saturn's B ring.

▶**Solar System Exploration: Saturn**

Learn about the Saturnian system from this NASA Web site. Information on the planet's atmosphere, history, rings, and moons is provided for you. Basic facts and figures are also available.

▶**The Story of Saturn**

This NASA site outlines our fascination with Saturn, beginning with the Assyrians in 700 B.C. and ending with the *Cassini-Huygens* mission. Information on some of the early astronomers who studied Saturn is also included.

▶**Titan**

Read about Titan and its unique atmosphere. Information on mapping this moon's surface and the *Cassini* spacecraft is provided.

▶**View of the Solar System: Saturn**

This Web site offers a lot of information on Saturn, the second largest planet in the solar system. A chart of Saturn's moons and the astronomers who discovered them is featured.

▶**Voyager: The Interstellar Mission**

Voyagers 1 and *2* were launched in 1977 on a mission to Jupiter, Saturn, Uranus, and Neptune. On this site, you can view images taken by each spacecraft and learn about the exploration of interstellar space.

▶**Windows to the Universe: Saturn**

This Web site provides information on Saturn's moons, rings, atmosphere, and magnetosphere.

Any comments? Contact us: **comments@myreportlinks.com**

Saturn Facts

Age
About 4.5 billion years

Diameter
74,600 miles (120,000 kilometers)

Composition
Giant ball of liquid and gas with a core made of molten rock or a hot rock-ice mixture

Average Distance From the Sun
877 million miles (1.4 billion kilometers)

Distances From Earth
741 million miles (1.2 billion kilometers) at its closest approach; 1 billion miles (1.7 billion kilometers) at its farthest passage

Orbital Period (year, in Earth years)
29 years, 167 days

Rotational Period (day, in Earth hours)
10 hours, 40 minutes

Atmosphere
96 percent hydrogen, 3 percent helium, and trace amounts of other gases, including methane, ammonia, and water vapor

Average Temperatures
Top of clouds: about −300°F (−184°C)
Outer core: 21,700°F (12,055°C)

Diameter of Rings
298,000 miles (480,000 kilometers)

Number of Known Moons
Thirty-three

Chapter 1

The Jewel of the Solar System

Saturn, the sixth planet from the Sun, is the second largest planet in the solar system. Compared to Earth, which has a diameter of 7,926 miles (12,753 kilometers), Saturn is a gigantic world. Its diameter at the equator measures 74,600 miles (120,000 kilometers). About 844 Earths could fit inside Saturn.

Saturn is a very different sort of world than Earth. While Earth and the other inner planets of the solar system—Mercury, Venus, and Mars—are solid, rocky objects, Saturn is mainly a giant ball of liquid and gas. Like the other outer planets—the gas giants Jupiter, Uranus, and Neptune—Saturn does not have a solid surface.

Many people have long considered Saturn and its spectacular system of rings to be a rare, exquisite jewel—the most beautiful and mysterious object that is visible in the night skies of Earth.

▲ *Jupiter, Saturn, Uranus, and Neptune are the four planets classified as gas giants.*

Although we now know that Jupiter, Neptune, and Uranus also have rings, those rings pale in comparison to Saturn's bright rings. Indeed, the other planets' rings are so dark, thin, and faint that they were only just discovered in recent years.

Saturn, Father of the Gods

Throughout most of human history, people believed that the planets and stars were either gods or goddesses. They also believed that all of the heavenly bodies revolved around Earth. But the ancient observers were able to distinguish between planets and stars. Five planets were visible to the naked eye—Mercury, Venus, Mars, Jupiter, and Saturn—and these were far brighter than the stars. The planets moved among the stars, which were situated in fixed patterns known as constellations. Witnessing this movement, the ancients, including the Babylonians, Chinese, and Greeks, called the planets "wanderers." The Greek word *planetes* means "wanderer."

To the ancient Babylonians, Saturn was known as Ninib, the god of springtime and planting. The Egyptians believed Saturn to be Horus, the bull of heaven.[1] The Greeks called the planet Cronus, their god of agriculture, and father of the Olympian gods including Zeus (or the Roman god Jupiter). The Romans named the ringed planet Saturn after their god of agriculture, and that is the name we still use today. The Romans also celebrated a seven-day winter festival beginning on December 17, around the time of the winter solstice, known as the Saturnalia. It was based on ancient fertility rituals of the harvest.[2] The English word for the seventh day of the week, *Saturday,* comes from the Latin word *Saturnus* (Saturn) and the Old English word *daeg* (day).

The Universe of the Ancients

For thousands of years, most people believed that Earth was the center of the universe. Ancient astronomers assumed that all the heavenly bodies moved around a stationary Earth. The Sun

Cronus (Saturn)

In Greek mythology, Cronus was the son of Uranus and Gaea. He lead his brothers and sisters, the Titans, in a revolt against their father and became the king of the gods. He married the Titan Rhea.

They had a total of six children, but Cronus had a bad habit of eating his newborn children, to prevent them from one day overthrowing him as king of the gods. Finally, at the birth of her last child, Zeus, Rhea tricked him into swallowing a rock instead. Zeus then beat his father, with the help of his brothers and sisters. The Romans adopted Cronus as the god Saturn.

Drawing by Rei Inamoto.

Internet

The ancient Romans adopted the Greek god Cronus but called him Saturn. The sixth planet from the Sun is named for this figure from Roman mythology.

appeared to rise in the east, travel across the sky, and set in the west. The astronomers' own observations supported their beliefs, which came to be known as the geocentric, or Earth-centered, theory of the universe.

A very different notion about the world was proposed by the ancient Greek astronomer Aristarchus of Samos in the third century B.C. Aristarchus became convinced that it was the Sun, not Earth, that was at the center of the solar system. He believed that the Sun was much larger than Earth, and that all the planets, including Earth, revolved around the Sun. Most people at the time believed that Aristarchus' heliocentric, or Sun-centered, theory defied common sense, so they ignored his ideas. After all, nobody could actually feel Earth's movements as it rotated on its axis and revolved around the Sun. The famous Alexandrian Greek astronomer Claudius Ptolemy wrote so convincingly in support of an Earth-centered universe that that view remained unchallenged for almost the next fifteen hundred years.

The Copernican Revolution

In 1543, the Polish astronomer Nicolaus Copernicus published *On the Revolutions of the Celestial Spheres.* In it, he presented his argument in support of the heliocentric theory. Copernicus, who knew about Aristarchus and his ideas, thought that the ancient Greek astronomer had stumbled onto the truth. After conducting his own careful study of the heavens, Copernicus came to the conclusion that Aristarchus was right. It was because of Copernicus' persuasive arguments for a heliocentric model, along with the convincing

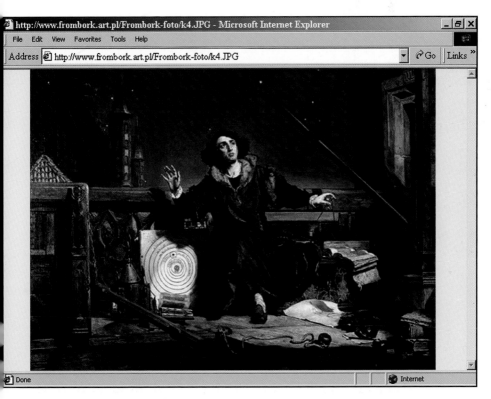

▲ *Nicolaus Copernicus argued for a Sun-centered model of the universe.*

evidence provided later by astronomers like Galileo Galilei and Johannes Kepler, that people eventually accepted as fact that Earth and the other planets revolve around the Sun.

Galileo Looks at Saturn

In July 1610, the Italian astronomer Galileo Galilei became the first person to look at Saturn through a telescope. He observed the planet as a yellowish disk with what appeared to be handles on each side. Galileo assumed Saturn's handles to be a satellite, or moon, on either side of the planet. He told the duke of Tuscany, "I have discovered a most extraordinary marvel. . . . The fact is that the planet Saturn is not one alone, but is composed of three, which almost touch one another and never move nor change with respect to one another."[3]

Several months earlier, Galileo had discovered four moons that revolved around Jupiter, and these later came to be known as the Galilean moons. He believed that this discovery would give strong support to Copernicus' heliocentric ideas. The existence of Saturnian moons would only strengthen the Copernican theory.

Moons . . . or Rings?

But soon there was a problem with Galileo's two Saturnian moons: Just two years later, he could no longer find them. He was extremely puzzled by this development. He wrote, "How can this be? . . . Have they suddenly vanished and fled? Or has Saturn devoured his own children? Or was the appearance a fraud and illusion? I cannot resolve so new, so strange, so unexpected a change. The shortness of time, the weakness of my intellect, the terror of being mistaken, have greatly confounded me."[4]

Galileo need not have worried. His "moons" had not disappeared because they were not moons to begin with. Although Galileo did not know it at the time, he had actually observed Saturn and its system of rings. In 1655, the Dutch astronomer Christiaan Huygens observed Saturn through a more powerful

ESA - Science - People - Discoverer of Titan: Christiaan Huygens - Microsoft Internet Explorer

File   Edit   View   Favorites   Tools   Help

Address http://www.esa.int/esaSC/SEMJRT57ESD_people_1.html   Go   Links »

Science missions

Multimedia
Multimedia gallery
Resources
Reference section
Glossary
FAQs
Downloads
Sounds from space
Services
Calendar
Help
Legal disclaimer
Subscribers
Search
  ○ All
  ● Space Science
                    GO
Advanced Search

Article Images

Discoverer of Titan: Christiaan Huygens

« Back to article

Exploring Saturn and Titan

More about...
• Cassini-Huygens factsheet
Related articles
• No rest on the way to the most mysterious of Saturn's moons
• Splashing down on Titan's oceans
• Challenges of landing on alien worlds
• ESA to search for life, but not as we know it
• Astrology to astronomy: Jean-Dominique Cassini
Related links
• NASA's Cassini-Huygens site
• Italian Space Agency (ASI)

Internet

The Dutch astronomer Christiaan Huygens discovered Saturn's moon Titan in 1655.

telescope and discovered the planet's largest moon, Titan. He also announced that the planet was surrounded "by a thin, flat ring, nowhere touching, and inclined to the ecliptic [the plane in which Earth orbits the Sun]."[5] Huygens calculated that every fifteen years, only the edges of Saturn's rings were visible from Earth. At these times, the thin rings would become almost invisible, which explains why Galileo's "moons" had seemed to disappear.

Over the next few hundred years, more powerful telescopes were developed, and astronomers observing Saturn continued to learn more about the planet and its system of rings and moons. In 1675, the Italian astronomer Giovanni Domenico Cassini observed a dark line that divided the rings. Today that gap in the rings is called the Cassini Division in honor of its discoverer.

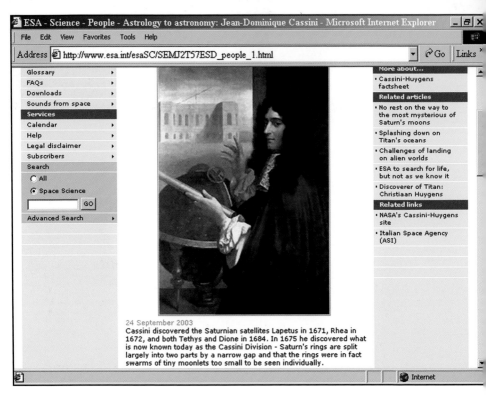

▲ *In 1675, Giovanni Cassini discovered a gap in Saturn's rings. That gap is now called the Cassini Division in his honor.*

Cassini also discovered Saturn's moons Iapetus in 1671, Rhea in 1672, and Dione and Tethys in 1684.

Astronomers continued to find more moons orbiting Saturn. In 1789, the British astronomer Sir William Herschel discovered Mimas and Enceladus. In 1848, the American astronomer George Bond discovered Hyperion. In 1898, the American astronomer William Pickering discovered Phoebe. And in 1966, the French astronomer Audouin Dollfus discovered Janus. In the late twentieth century and early twenty-first century, unmanned space probes were launched to the outer planets of the solar system. Their findings led to new discoveries about Saturn and its system of rings and moons.

Chapter 2

The Ringed Planet

Although Saturn is only about 85 percent the size of Jupiter, the largest planet, Saturn is still a true giant, ninety-five times as massive as Earth. Like Jupiter, Saturn is a huge ball of liquid and gas. And like Jupiter, Saturn has an extremely powerful magnetic field. Although Jupiter's magnetic field is ten times as large as Saturn's, Saturn's magnetic field, or magnetosphere, still may extend over a million miles. It is about one thousand times more powerful than Earth's magnetic field. Despite the ringed planet's great mass, its "surface" gravity is only about 92 percent of Earth's.

Amazingly, for such a large planet, Saturn has a very low density, the lowest of any planet in the solar system. That is why the planet has such a low surface gravity. Indeed, Saturn's density is only about seven tenths the density of water. If there were a gigantic body of water large enough to swallow Saturn, the ringed planet is so light that it would float on top.[1]

The Cassini spacecraft took ▶ this colorful image of Saturn's many-hued atmospheric bands in May 2004.

How Saturn Was Formed

Scientists believe that the solar system formed about 4.5 billion years ago. Gases and dust particles floating in a "protostellar nebula" between the stars were pulled together by their own gravitational forces into a spinning disk. The Sun formed first at the center of the disk. The planets formed soon after that from gas, dust, and clumps of rocky debris circling the Sun.

Earth and the other inner planets formed in the warm inner part of the disk closest to the Sun. Farther out from the Sun in a much colder part of the disk, icy chunks of rock and frozen gases formed larger planets. Hydrogen and helium gases were blown outward by the Sun from the inner part of the solar system. A huge gas cloud formed around the icy outer planets. These planets, the gas giants, continued to grow even larger as their gravity attracted more and more gases. Jupiter and Saturn became the largest planets because they were situated in the thickest part of the gas cloud and they attracted the most gas.

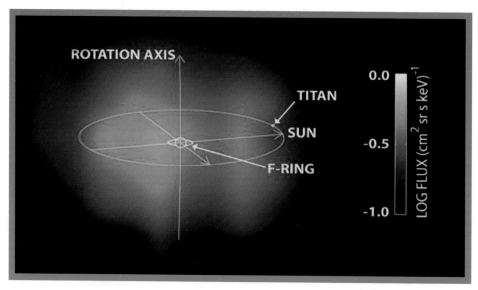

▲ Cassini *also captured this image of Saturn's magnetosphere in 2004. This area of charged particles is invisible to the naked eye, but an imaging instrument on board the spacecraft was able to detect hydrogen atoms escaping from the magnetic field.*

Because Saturn is so much farther away from the Sun than Earth is, the ringed planet receives only about one percent of the amount of heat that Earth gets from the Sun. Yet, Saturn is not as cold as you might expect. Like Jupiter, Saturn has its own internal source of heat energy and gives off almost twice as much heat as it receives from the Sun. Saturn and Jupiter were even larger and hotter when they first formed, although they were not nearly massive enough to trigger thermonuclear fusion, the process that powers the Sun. As the two planets cooled and contracted, heat energy was stored in their interiors. Gravitational energy was converted to heat as particles of matter fell inward and collided with each other. This process is still happening with Jupiter, but Saturn generates its internal heat by a different process: Its helium produces heat by friction as it falls through the hydrogen.

Saturn's Atmosphere

Saturn's atmosphere is composed of 96 percent hydrogen, 3 percent helium, and trace amounts of other gases, including methane, ammonia, water vapor, and hydrogen sulfide. There are three cloud layers in the atmosphere. The top layer consists of ammonia ice crystals. The temperature at the top of this layer is a frigid $-300°F$ ($-184°C$). The middle layer consists of clouds of ammonium hydrosulfide. And the bottom layer consists of water ice crystals or droplets.

Because of radio noise picked up by the *Cassini* spacecraft, which was launched in October 1997 and entered Saturn's orbit in June 2004, we now know that powerful lightning storms appear in Saturn's atmosphere, as they also do in Jupiter's.

Saturn's bands of yellowish clouds are constantly moving. The cloud bands move parallel to the planet's equator. Saturn's rapid rate of rotation causes the bands of clouds to whip around the planet at enormous speeds. Wind speeds as high as 1,100 miles per hour (1,770 kilometers per hour) have been measured in Saturn's upper atmosphere at the equator. The lighter bands are

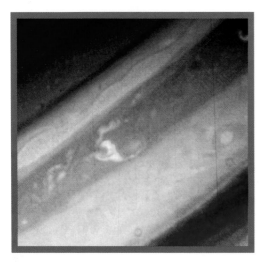

Color has been added to this Voyager image of Saturn's northern hemisphere to highlight cloud features in different belts and regions of the planet.

called zones and the darker ones are called belts. Some cloud bands move west to east, while others move east to west.

Turbulent weather is common where adjacent bands moving in opposite directions meet. Huge hurricane-like storms appear as white, brown, or red oval patches. Spectacular white spots have been recorded in Saturn's northern hemisphere about once every thirty years. Although the storms on Saturn are not nearly as common or as large as those on Jupiter, there is a big red spot called Anne's Spot in Saturn's southern hemisphere. It was named after Anne Bunker, a scientist who worked on the Voyager space probe missions. Anne's Spot measures about 3,000 by 2,000 miles (5,000 by 3,000 kilometers), which is small when compared with Jupiter's 25,000-mile-wide (40,000-kilometer-wide) Great Red Spot. The reddish color comes from phosphorus.[2] A huge white spot in Saturn's northern hemisphere, called Big Bertha, measures about 6,000 by 3,700 miles (10,000 by 6,000 kilometers). As on Jupiter, Saturn's storms are sustained by heat from the planet's interior.

Saturn's Structure

Temperatures and pressures inside Saturn increase with depth, causing the hydrogen gas to become liquid hydrogen. Scientists believe that Saturn is completely covered by a vast liquid hydrogen ocean that may be tens of thousands of miles deep. Beneath this layer, pressures are so great that the liquid hydrogen turns into liquid metallic hydrogen. The transition to liquid metallic hydrogen occurs about halfway from the cloud tops to the center of the planet. This layer is where Saturn's strong magnetic field is generated, just as Jupiter's magnetic field is.

Below this layer of liquid metallic hydrogen is Saturn's relatively small, dense core at the center of the planet. Although Saturn's core is small in comparison to the planet's total size, the core itself is about as large as Earth.

The core may be made of melted rock or a hot rock-ice mixture. The ice stays solid here because of the extremely high pressure being exerted on the core, which is 12 million times the pressure on Earth's surface. Temperatures at the outer core can climb as high as 21,700°F (12,055°C).

These images of Saturn show ▷ *the planet's rings opening up as Saturn moved from autumn to winter.*

▷ The Movements of Saturn

Saturn is about twice as far from our own planet as Jupiter is. The ringed planet's distance from Earth ranges from 741 million miles (1.2 billion kilometers) at its closest approach to 1 billion miles (1.7 billion kilometers) at its farthest passage. Saturn's average distance from the Sun is about 877 million miles (1.4 billion kilometers).

Because Saturn is so much farther away from the Sun than Earth is, the ringed planet takes much longer than Earth to complete its orbit around the Sun. Earth takes 365 days, or one year, to complete one revolution around the Sun. But Saturn takes nearly thirty Earth years to travel around the Sun.

As Saturn revolves around the Sun, it rotates on its axis. Saturn's axis is tilted at an angle of 26.7 degrees from the plane of its orbit. This allows astronomers on Earth to get different views of Saturn's rings as the planet revolves around the Sun. While Earth takes just under twenty-four hours, or one day, to make a complete rotation, Saturn spins around in ten hours and forty minutes, faster than any other planet except Jupiter. Saturn's rapid rotation causes the planet to bulge outward at its equator. It also drives electrical currents in the liquid metallic hydrogen in Saturn's interior. Scientists believe these currents produce the planet's powerful magnetic field.

Chapter 3

Saturn's Mysterious Rings

The first astronomers to study Saturn through a telescope did not know where the planet's magnificent rings had come from or what they were made of. Some believed the rings were made of solid rock, while others later wondered whether they might be made of liquid or gas. It was not until recently that we learned the true nature of the rings.

▷ Trillions and Trillions of Ice Particles

At first, most astronomers believed that Saturn's rings were a solid object. But in 1795, the French mathematician Pierre-Simon Laplace calculated that Saturn's rings could not possibly be solid because they would be broken up by the gravitational forces of the giant planet. He thought that the rings were probably divided into thousands of very narrow rings. The British astronomer Sir William Herschel also proposed that the rings were extremely thin because they disappeared from view at times, and when Saturn passed close to a star, the star could sometimes be seen through the rings.

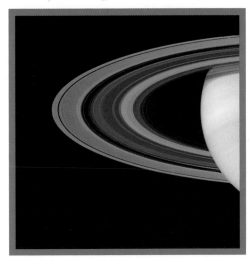

The color differences in this striking ▷ image of Saturn's rings reflect changes in their temperatures.

In 1850, a new ring was discovered inside the other two rings by American astronomers William C. Bond and George P. Bond, father and son, and English astronomer William Rutter Dawes. The new ring came to be called the crepe ring because it was extremely thin and transparent enough so that Saturn could be seen through it. This discovery proved that at least one of Saturn's rings was not a solid body. But scientists did not yet know just what the rings were made of.

In 1857, the Scottish physicist James Clerk Maxwell, inspired by the ideas of Laplace, calculated that any solid ring around Saturn, even the thinnest ring possible, would be torn apart by the planet's gravitational forces. In 1895, the American astronomer James E. Keeler confirmed Maxwell's theory by measuring the rotational speed of different parts of the rings. Using a spectroscope to examine the light from the rings, Keeler found that the inner parts rotated faster than the outer parts, taking seven hours compared to twenty-two hours.[1] This could only be true if the rings were made up of individual particles.

Today, thanks in part to radar observations and data sent back to Earth from unmanned space probes, we know that Saturn's rings are made up of trillions of individual particles of water ice. Some of the ice particles are coated with dust and resemble dirty snowballs. Just like a moon, each particle moves in its own orbit around Saturn. Some of the particles are as small as a grain of sand, while others can range up to a half-mile across. Some chunks of ice in the rings may be even larger.

▶ A Complex System of Rings

In 1837, the German astronomer Johann Franz Encke discovered a gap dividing the outer ring into two parts. So now there was an Encke Division in addition to the Cassini Division. With each new discovery, scientists became more aware of how complex Saturn's ring system truly was.

The ring system occupies a vast area of space. It extends for more than 298,000 miles (480,000 kilometers). Amazingly, the rings are so thin that their thicknesses range from about 33 to 660 feet (10 to 200 meters).[2] Astronomers have used letters of the alphabet, corresponding with the order of their discovery, to name the main rings. The Cassini Division separates the A and B rings. The so-called crepe ring is known as the C ring. In addition to the three main rings are four others—D, E, F, and G. The D ring is closest to Saturn, then come the C, B, A, F, G, and E rings. The recently discovered Titan ringlet and Maxwell ringlet lie between the C and B rings.

The rings vary in width, brightness, and density. The Voyager unmanned space probe missions revealed that the main rings are made up of one thousand or more ringlets. Laplace's theory about ringlets turned out to be correct. Some of the ringlets look as if they are braided together. The B ring, the brightest and densest of

This image of Saturn's A ring, seen from the inside out, indicates that there is more ice toward the outer part of the rings than in the inner part. The Cassini Division followed by the A ring is the faint red area at the left.

the rings, is about 16,000 miles (25,500 kilometers) wide. It is so opaque (not penetrated by light) that it casts a shadow on Saturn. Dark lines, like spokes on a wheel, have been observed from time to time on the B ring. The spokes are believed to have formed when dust particles were affected by electromagnetic activity in Saturn's magnetic field.

The A ring is about 9,100 miles (14,600 kilometers) wide. The Cassini Division separating the A and B rings is about 2,900 miles (4,700 kilometers) wide. The C ring is about eleven thousand miles (17,500 kilometers) wide. The narrow Maxwell Division (named for James Clerk Maxwell) separating the B ring and the C ring is 300 miles (483 kilometers) wide.

At a distance of 4,200 miles (6,758 kilometers) from the cloud tops of Saturn, the faint D ring is the closest to the planet. Indeed, the 4,700-mile-wide (7,500-kilometer-wide) ring is so close that its inner edge may touch Saturn's atmosphere. The narrow F ring, located beyond the A ring, is between 20 and 310 miles (30 and 500 kilometers) wide. The *Cassini* spacecraft has detected a faint ring between the A and F rings. Farther out are the faint G and E rings. The E ring, which is about 14,900 miles (24,000 kilometers) wide, is about 260,000 miles (420,000 kilometers) above Saturn's cloud tops.

Scientists believe that the gaps in Saturn's rings were caused by the gravitational forces of the planet's moons. Some of these satellites, known as shepherd satellites, follow orbits that are very close to the rings. Other satellites are actually embedded in the rings. The satellites' gravity affects the orbits of the individual particles in the rings, forcing the particles into narrow rings. The Cassini Division was probably caused by the gravitational pull of Saturn's moon Mimas.[3]

▶ How the Rings Were Formed

Astronomers have several theories to explain how and when Saturn's rings formed. Some of these theories are related to the ideas of a French mathematician named Edouard Roche. In 1850, Roche proposed that there is a zone around any planet in which the planet's gravitational forces will tear apart a moon or another object that wanders too close. This distance is known as the Roche limit. And Saturn's rings happen to be mostly situated in this zone.

Scientists believe it is possible that a huge icy object from the outer edge of the solar system wandered too close to Saturn, into the planet's Roche limit, and was pulled apart by the planet's gravity. It is even possible that one of Saturn's own moons drifted too close to the planet and was ripped apart. In either case, the resulting debris could have formed rings around the planet.

Another possibility is that one of Saturn's moons may have been struck by a comet or asteroid whose impact blew the moon to bits, with the resulting particles going into orbit around Saturn. The planet's gravity was too strong to allow the particles

△ *On October 15, 1997, the* Cassini *spacecraft, with the* Huygens *probe attached, was launched from Cape Canaveral, Florida, on its seven-year journey to Saturn.*

to come together and form a moon again, forcing them into a permanent system of rings.

According to another theory, when Saturn was formed, some material orbiting the planet may have failed to come together to form a moon and instead became the rings.

Later Theories

Today, though, many scientists think that Saturn's rings are not nearly as old as the planet and may be much younger. Dust in space is constantly falling on every object in the solar system. But Saturn's rings are bright, indicating that they were not exposed to the dust long enough to have darkened.

Most scientists now think that it is possible that the rings were formed from debris when two of Saturn's moons collided only a few thousand years ago. The rings of the other gas giants may have formed the same way but much longer ago and have mostly disappeared by being pulled into the outer layers of these planets. Scientists predict that Saturn, too, may lose its rings— but not for 100 million years or so.

Scientists hope that an analysis of data from the *Cassini* space probe, which is now orbiting Saturn, will provide more clues about the origin and composition of the rings. The individual particles that make up the rings mainly consist of water ice, but perhaps as much as 10 percent may consist of other substances such as carbon, ammonia, or organic compounds. These may be responsible for the pink, gray, and brown colors of the rings as seen by *Cassini,* which has also shown us that oxygen atoms form a huge cloud around Saturn. The cloud comes from moonlets in the rings that are constantly colliding, producing ice fragments. The ice fragments are bombarded by particles trapped in Saturn's magnetic field, which releases the oxygen atoms.

Once scientists better understand what the rings are made of, they may be able to determine which theory best explains how and when the rings came to be.

The Moons of Saturn

Saturn and its complex system of rings and moons are like a miniature solar system. There are thirty-three known moons revolving around Saturn, including two that were recently discovered by *Cassini*. It is very possible that Saturn has even more moons. Eighteen of the moons have officially been named, while unofficial names and numbers have been assigned to the rest.

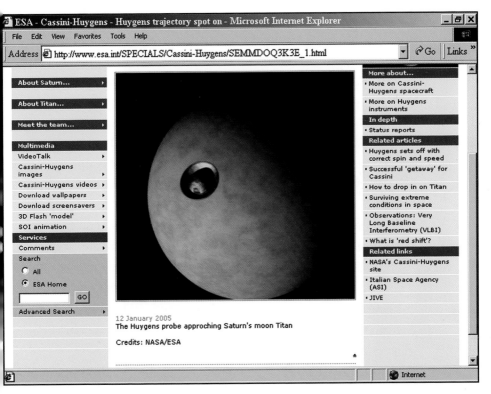

🔺 *The saucer-shaped* Huygens *probe is seen as it approached Titan in January 2005 before touching down on the huge Saturnian moon.*

Almost all of Saturn's moons make one rotation during the time it takes them to complete one revolution around the planet. Like Earth's Moon, these moons always keep the same side facing Saturn. Some follow orbits very close to the planet, while others orbit far out in space. And some of Saturn's moons are situated within Saturn's rings. While most of Saturn's moons are small icy bodies, Titan is a very different sort of world.

▷ Titan

Titan, discovered in 1655 by Christiaan Huygens, orbits Saturn at a distance of 697,118 miles (1,121,850 kilometers). Titan, larger than Earth's Moon, is huge. It is even larger than the planets Mercury and Pluto. With a diameter of 3,200 miles (5,150 kilometers), Titan is the second largest moon in the solar system, nearly as big as Jupiter's moon Ganymede. While Titan's size is impressive, there is something else about this giant moon that intrigues scientists: Titan is the only moon in the solar system known to have a thick atmosphere. The satellite's atmosphere was discovered in 1944 by the Dutch-American astronomer Gerard P. Kuiper. Scientists are also intrigued by this Saturnian moon because they believe that the conditions on Titan may be very similar to the ancient chemical environment, the "organic soup," that existed on Earth when life first emerged, about 4 billion years ago. And after a probe made a historic landing on Titan in 2005, scientists were excited to discover that Titan is, even now, like our own planet in some very important ways.

▷ Titan "Rediscovered" by Another *Huygens*

In January 2005, scientists began to learn much more about Saturn's largest moon when the *Huygens* probe, part of the *Cassini-Huygens* mission to Saturn, parachuted safely down to the muddy, frozen surface of Titan. And what they found was that the once-mysterious moon was even more like Earth than they had thought.

The early images captured by *Huygens* revealed a world that is very much like our own meteorologically and geologically. Images taken by cameras aboard the *Huygens* probe reveal liquid on Titan in the form of methane. They also show a complex system of drainage channels that run from highland regions to flat lowlands and merge into river systems. These run into lake beds that feature offshore islands and shoals, like those on Earth. Although there appears to be no liquid in Titan's rivers or lakes now, there is evidence that methane rain may have fallen there not long ago.

Scientists now know that Titan's landscape, like Earth's landscape, has been affected by erosion and volcanic activity. The difference is that when volcanoes erupted on Titan, where temperatures average −292°F (−180°C), they spewed water ice and ammonia instead of hot lava. Scientists also found that the Titanian soil, made up mostly of dirty water ice and hydrocarbon ice, is darker than they had expected.

▷ A Hazy Atmosphere

At the surface, Titan's atmosphere is four times denser than Earth's, but because Titan's gravity is weaker, its atmospheric pressure is only about 50 percent greater than Earth's.[1] The weaker gravity also explains why Titan's atmosphere extends ten times farther into space than Earth's atmosphere does.

Before the *Huygens* probe landed, scientists thought that Titan's atmosphere, like Earth's atmosphere, consisted mostly

The Huygens *probe captured this historic first* ▷ *color image of Titan and its pebble-sized surface features on January 14, 2005, when it became the first spacecraft to land on another planet's moon.*

of nitrogen, making Titan and Earth the only two bodies in the solar system with significant atmospheres that mainly consist of nitrogen. (Pluto and Neptune's moon Triton also have nitrogen atmospheres, but very thin ones.) The instruments on *Huygens* found that Titan's atmosphere at about 100 miles (160 kilometers) above the surface was a uniform mix of nitrogen and methane, with methane becoming more concentrated closer to the ground. Clouds of methane and ethane fog were detected near Titan's surface.

A Huge Ball Enveloped in Orange Smog

Titan looks like an orange ball floating in the blackness of space because a dense orange smog completely obscures its surface. Scientists think that the smog is caused by sunlight acting on nitrogen and methane to form molecules known as tholins. There are many complex organic molecules (molecules containing carbon) on Titan. Rain on Titan may fall in the form of hydrocarbons, condensing out of the atmosphere and falling onto the extremely cold surface of this moon.

It is possible that some sort of microbial life could have existed on Titan that was like life-forms that exist in extreme environments on Earth, such as those in the deepest parts of the oceans. When Christiaan Huygens discovered Titan, he knew much less about conditions on this large moon than today's scientists do. But he thought it possible that the moons of Saturn were inhabited by some kind of life-form. He was aware that the seasons on Saturn and its moons are much longer than those on Earth because Saturn takes thirty years to revolve around the Sun. This led Huygens to speculate that for any inhabitants of Saturn's moons, "It is impossible but that their way of living must be very different from ours, having such tedious Winters."[2]

Saturn's Other Large Satellites

Saturn's six other large satellites are all spherical objects made of water ice and rock. Some of them may have a rocky core. Five

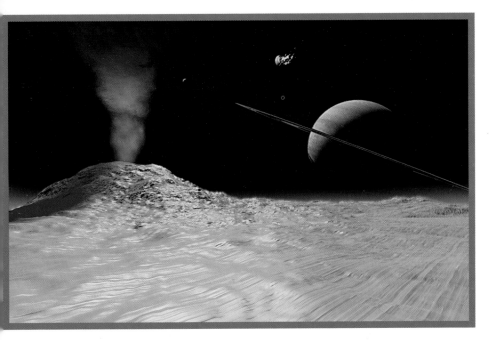

An artist's idea of what the icy surface of Enceladus might look like, complete with a spouting ice geyser. Scientists think that this moon might be the source of the particles that make up Saturn's E ring.

of them—Mimas, Enceladus, Tethys, Dione, and Rhea—orbit Saturn closely beyond the ring system. Iapetus is much farther out, beyond the orbit of Hyperion, a smaller Saturnian moon.

Mimas, the closest of this group, orbits Saturn at a distance of 115,282 miles (185,520 kilometers) and has a diameter of 240 miles (390 kilometers). Its heavily cratered surface bears a resemblance to Earth's Moon. Scientists believe the extensive cratering was a result of Mimas's relative closeness to Saturn. The planet's gravitational forces pulled in passing meteoroids and asteroids, and many of these collided with Mimas. A huge impact crater called Herschel, named after Mimas's discoverer, is almost one-third the diameter of Mimas. It is 80 miles (130 kilometers) wide and about 5.6 miles (9 kilometers) deep. If the impact had been any bigger, Mimas probably would have shattered.

Enceladus, with a diameter of 311 miles (500 kilometers), orbits Saturn at a distance of 147,906 miles (238,020 kilometers). Scientists believe Enceladus is made up almost completely of pure water ice because it reflects almost 100 percent of the sunlight reaching it. In fact, Enceladus is the most reflective object in the solar system. In comparison, Earth's Moon reflects only about 11 percent of the sunlight that falls on it. Unlike Mimas, which is almost totally covered by craters, only one hemisphere of Enceladus has much cratering. The other hemisphere is smooth except for narrow grooves and cracks. Astronomers believe the ice there may have fractured when it melted and then froze over again.

Tethys is 183,102 miles (294,660 kilometers) from Saturn and has a diameter of 659 miles (1,060 kilometers). It is heavily cratered but also has some smooth areas. Odysseus, one of its craters, is so large, 250 miles (400 kilometers) across, that the moon Mimas could fit inside it. There is a huge valley system on Tethys, known as Ithaca Chasma, that stretches 1,243 miles (2,000 kilometers) across the surface, about three quarters of the way around the satellite. Ithaca Chasma is 62 miles (100 kilometers) wide and 2 to 3 miles (3 to 5 kilometers) deep. Scientists believe it could have been formed by fracturing of the crust following the same impact that caused the Odysseus Crater.

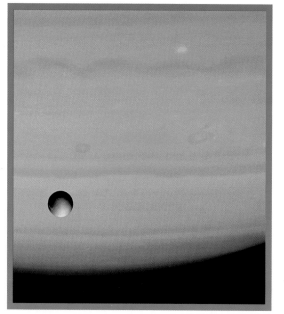

◁ A tiny Dione is photographed against the globe of Saturn as the planet and its moon came close in December 2004. Dione appears to lack the rich atmospheric hues of its host planet.

▲ Landslides are common occurrences on many planets and their moons. This landslide was photographed in the Cassini Regio region of Iapetus, one of Saturn's distant moons.

Dione, with a diameter of 700 miles (1,120 kilometers), is 234,516 miles (377,400 kilometers) from Saturn. One hemisphere is heavily cratered, while the other side is darker and has fewer craters. The darker side has bright, wispy streaks on top of some of the craters. The streaks might be deposits of ice, caused by water that flowed into cracks on the surface. Dione is about the same size as Tethys, but it is denser and most likely contains more rocky material. There are large valleys, hundreds of miles long and more than 10 miles (16 kilometers) wide.

Rhea, Saturn's second largest satellite, has a diameter of 950 miles (1,530 kilometers) and orbits Saturn at a distance of 327,503 miles (527, 040 kilometers). Rhea is made mostly of ice and has a very low density. Like Dione, one of Rhea's hemispheres is heavily cratered. Also like Dione, the other hemisphere is darker and has bright, wispy streaks.

Iapetus is far from Saturn, at a distance of 2.2 million miles (3.5 million kilometers). It is almost as large as Rhea, with a diameter of 908 miles (1,460 kilometers). One side of Iapetus is bright and cratered. But the other side is so much darker, at least ten times darker, that Iapetus sometimes seems to disappear from view. The dark side appears to be coated with a reddish-brown substance, possibly organic compounds. Some scientists think the material may have been deposited by a comet or picked up by Iapetus as particles ejected from the moon Phoebe. Others believe the material could have erupted volcanically from the interior of Iapetus because it also seems to be present in the floors of craters on the other side of the satellite. The mystery may be solved when *Cassini* makes its two scheduled close flybys of Iapetus in the next few years.

▶ The Minor Satellites

Phoebe, a spherical object with a diameter of about 137 miles (220 kilometers), is the largest of Saturn's minor moons. It is also one of the planet's most distant satellites, orbiting Saturn at 8 million miles (13 million kilometers). Unlike the other moons that orbit Saturn from east to west, Phoebe orbits in a retrograde, or opposite, direction. Because of this and its great distance from Saturn, scientists think that Phoebe may have wandered too close to Saturn and was captured by the planet's gravity. Like Iapetus, Phoebe's surface is coated with a dark material that may be organic. The most recent data from *Cassini,* shows Phoebe to be an icy body with a surface of water ice, frozen carbon dioxide, minerals, and solid hydrocarbons. Its surface temperature is $-261°F$ ($-163°C$). This data suggests that Phoebe was probably formed in the Kuiper Belt (the disk-shaped region beyond Neptune where Pluto and other icy bodies are located) and then moved in to be captured by Saturn.

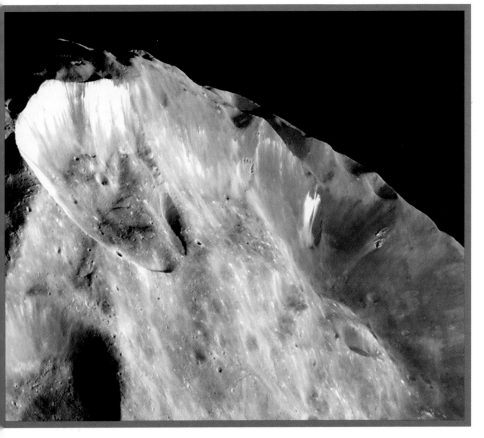

△ *On June 11, 2004,* Cassini *took this close-up image of a crater on Phoebe.* Cassini *came within 1,285 miles (2,068 kilometers) of the tiny Saturnian moon. Voyager 2, in 1981, had been the last probe to fly by Phoebe—but it did so from a distance of one thousand times farther away.*

Hyperion and all of the other smaller satellites have irregular shapes. They could be fragments of larger bodies that broke apart when they collided with asteroids or other objects. Hyperion, which has been described as being shaped like a hamburger patty, has a diameter of 180 miles (290 kilometers) and orbits Saturn at a distance of 920,356 miles (1.4 million kilometers). Hyperion and Phoebe are the only satellites that do not always keep the same side facing Saturn. The main feature on the surface of Hyperion is a crater that is 62 miles (100 kilometers) wide.

▷ Shepherds and Co-orbitals

Two pairs of moons—Pan and Atlas, and Prometheus and Pandora—are known as "shepherd" satellites because of their relationship with Saturn's rings. Like a shepherd herding a flock of sheep, the shepherd satellites "herd" the particles in the ring. The gravitational forces of the shepherd satellites keep the particles within a ring by pulling stragglers back in, maintaining the ring's structure. Pan and Atlas are small rocky lumps that orbit close to the edge of the A ring, with one moon on each side of the ring. Prometheus and Pandora orbit alongside the F ring, also with one moon on each side.

Janus and Epimetheus are known as co-orbital satellites because they share practically the same orbit around Saturn, their minimum separation being only 30 miles (50 kilometers) apart. They travel at slightly different speeds. Every four years the faster moving satellite catches up with the slower moving one. Their gravitational pull then causes them to exchange orbits. Scientists have not witnessed this phenomenon anywhere else in the solar system, and they think that the two co-orbital moons were formed when a larger satellite broke apart.

▷ Lagrangian Satellites

Calypso, Helene, and Telesto are known as Lagrangian satellites because they are located at points in larger moons' orbits known as Lagrangian points. The eighteenth-century French mathematician Joseph-Louis Lagrange showed that it is possible for a smaller object to share the orbit of a moon or planet if it is situated 60 degrees behind or in front of the larger object. Calypso and Telesto are at the two Lagrangian points in the orbit of Tethys. Helene is located at one Lagrangian point in the orbit of Dione.

Chapter 5 ▶

The Exploration of Saturn

A great leap forward in our understanding of Saturn came with the launching of unmanned space probes to the ringed planet. During the decades of the Cold War between the United States and the Soviet Union, the exploration of space became a priority of both superpowers. In 1957, the Soviet Union launched *Sputnik,* the first unmanned satellite to successfully orbit Earth.

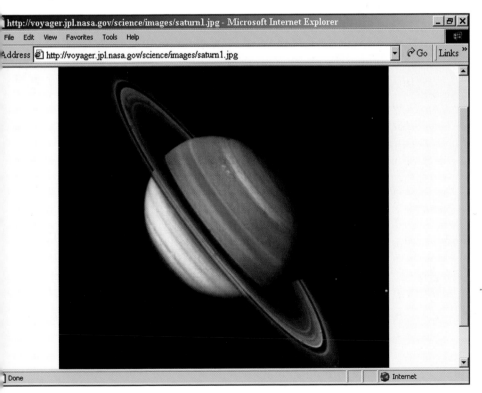

http://voyager.jpl.nasa.gov/science/images/saturn1.jpg - Microsoft Internet Explorer

File   Edit   View   Favorites   Tools   Help

Address   http://voyager.jpl.nasa.gov/science/images/saturn1.jpg   Go   Links

Done   Internet

△ The Voyager probes were the first to capture stunning images of Saturn's complex ring system.

This achievement caught the United States by surprise, and the Americans scrambled to catch up with the Russians in space. Both nations forged ahead with their own space programs in a race to the Moon. On July 20, 1969, the race was over when *Apollo 11* astronauts Neil Armstrong and Buzz Aldrin landed on the Moon and walked on the lunar surface.

Although getting to the Moon was probably the most important immediate goal of the United States and the Soviet Union, these countries had other ambitious goals in space. Both nations began programs that employed unmanned space probes to explore the other planets of the solar system.

The Pioneer and Voyager Missions

In April 1973, NASA (the National Aeronautics and Space Administration) launched the *Pioneer 11* unmanned space probe. After flying by Jupiter in December 1974 and sending back data to Earth, *Pioneer 11* reached Saturn on September 1, 1979. *Pioneer 11* flew within 13,000 miles (21,000 kilometers) of the ringed planet and sent back the first close-up images of Saturn and its rings. Although the images were not very clear, they did give a sense of the complexity of the planet's ring system. The F ring was a major *Pioneer 11* discovery. *Pioneer 11* also sent back data about Saturn's magnetic field.

In 1977, NASA launched the *Voyager 1* and *Voyager 2* probes. *Voyager 1* flew by Saturn in November 1980 at a distance of 77,143 miles (124,123 kilometers). *Voyager 2* flew within 62,980 miles (101,335 kilometers) of Saturn in August 1981. While the cameras on *Pioneer 11* had been too slow to reveal much detail in Saturn's fast-moving clouds, the Voyager probes had much more sophisticated equipment. *Voyagers 1* and *2* sent back close-up images of the banded structure of Saturn's clouds and revealed complicated patterns of wind flow in the planet's atmosphere. Cameras aboard the probes also captured detailed images of storm systems in Saturn's atmosphere.

The Voyager images showed just how amazingly complex Saturn's ring system is by revealing rings made up of more than one thousand ringlets.[1] They also showed subtle color differences in the rings and in the clouds in the atmosphere.

Voyagers 1 and *2* also gave astronomers their first close-up views of many of Saturn's moons. In November 1980, *Voyager 1*

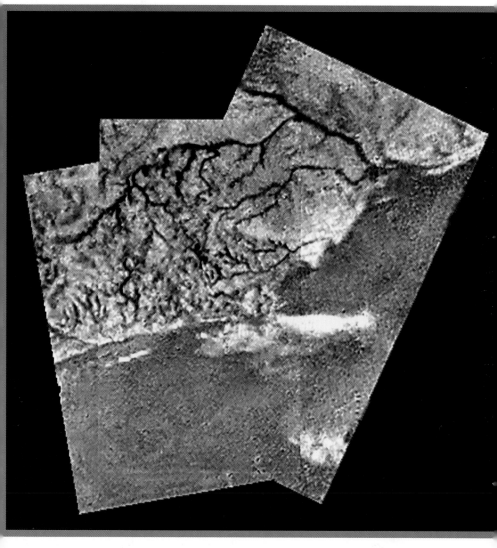

Scientists were thrilled with these early images of Titan because they appear to show a coastline and river channels not unlike those found on Earth.

flew by Titan at a distance of only 2,485 miles (4,000 kilometers) and sent back so much data that scientists are still analyzing it.[2] As scientists studied the many high-resolution images of Titan, they were unable to get even the barest glimpse of the surface. They quickly grasped that the entire moon was shrouded in a thick haze or smog. The scientists did, however, learn a great deal about the composition and density of Titan's atmosphere.[3]

▷ The *Cassini-Huygens* Mission

With Voyager, scientists learned much more about Saturn and its system of rings and moons than had ever been known before. But as often happens, new scientific discoveries led to new questions and the search for answers. Scientists were especially eager to learn more about Titan. After all, the new data suggested parallels between Titan's environment and Earth's environment in its early history when life first emerged. The next mission to Saturn would have to involve a spacecraft capable of orbiting the ringed planet for an extended period of time rather than another flyby like Voyager.

In October 1997, NASA launched the *Cassini-Huygens* orbiter and probe on a 2.2-billion-mile (3.5-billion-kilometer) journey to Saturn. The mission is named for Giovanni Cassini, the astronomer who identified the gap between Saturn's A ring and B ring and some of Saturn's moons, and Christiaan Huygens, the astronomer who discovered Titan and identified Saturn's ring system. The mission is a joint effort of three space agencies: NASA, the European Space Agency (ESA), and Agenzia Spaziale Italiana (ASI), the Italian space agency. The spacecraft consists of two parts: the *Cassini* orbiter, built and operated by NASA, and the *Huygens* probe, designed and controlled by European scientists.

▷ "A Grand Descent Into the Unknown"

After a nearly seven-year journey, *Cassini-Huygens* went into orbit around Saturn on June 30, 2004. It became the first spacecraft to orbit the ringed planet. The *Cassini* spacecraft's first flyby of Saturn's moon Titan came on October 26, 2004. (Forty-five more Titan flybys are planned for *Cassini*.) Then on December 24, 2004, the 11,550-pound (5,574-kilogram) *Cassini* successfully released the 740-pound (335-kilogram) *Huygens* probe on its solo journey to Titan. On January 14, 2005, the saucer-shaped probe parachuted for two-and-a-half hours through Titan's hazy atmosphere to land in a muddy area of the moon's frozen surface—a "grand descent into the unknown" in the words of Dr. David Southwood, the ESA's director of science programs.[4] European and American scientists were thrilled with the probe's safe landing on Titan, which became the first moon other than Earth's Moon to be explored.

Cassini moved into position around Saturn to receive radioed messages from *Huygens*, which began transmitting more than 350 images and significant data to the orbiting spacecraft 40,000 miles (64,000 kilometers) away. Scientists had thought that once *Huygens* landed on Titan, it would have enough power to send back data for at least a half-hour, but the probe continued to transmit data for more than two hours.

Early findings showed that Titan is a world not unlike our own, with river channels, highland areas, and signs of volcanic activity. But it is also very different from Earth. On Titan, liquid exists, but it is in the form of methane. Rocklike objects exist,

▽ The Huygens *probe took these images of Titan's landscape during its descent to the moon's surface.*

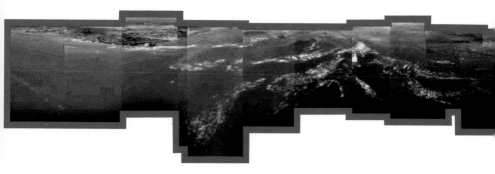

but instead of being made of silica, they are made of water ice. Volcanoes exist, but instead of erupting in lava, they erupted in ice.[5] Just a week after the probe touched down on the moon's surface, ESA scientist Dr. Martin Tomasko summed up the early findings this way:

> We now have the key to understanding what shapes Titan's landscape. . . . Geological evidence for precipitation, erosion, mechanical abrasion and other fluvial activity says that the physical processes shaping Titan are much the same as those shaping Earth.[6]

During the four years it orbits Saturn, *Cassini* will send back at least 750,000 photos of the planet and some of its moons. More than 250 scientists from Europe and North America will be studying the data received from the *Cassini-Huygens* mission for many years to come. There will undoubtedly be more unmanned missions to the ringed planet. And if any evidence of life is found on Titan, the next mission will probably occur sooner rather than later. The one thing we can be sure of is that Saturn will continue to fascinate us, even as more and more of its mysteries are solved.

asteroid—A small object (relative to the sizes of planets) made of rock or metal that revolves around the Sun.

atmosphere—The layer of gases around a star, planet, or moon.

comet—A ball of ice, frozen gases, and dust that orbits the Sun; a long tail forms when the Sun vaporizes some of the ice to release gases and dust.

co-orbital satellite—A moon that travels in the same orbit as another moon.

core—The center-most region of a planet or moon.

crust—The hard outer layer of a rocky or icy planet or moon.

gas giant—A large planet made up mainly of gas. The solar system has four gas giants: Jupiter, Saturn, Uranus, and Neptune.

gravity—The attraction or pull that every object has on other objects on or near it.

icy body—A small object made of ice and rocky material. Most icy bodies are in the Kuiper Belt, but some have been captured by the giant planets.

Kuiper Belt—A region beyond Neptune consisting of thousands of small icy bodies, of which Pluto is the largest.

magnetosphere—The area surrounding a planet where its magnetic force can be detected.

revolution—The movement of a planet in an orbit around the Sun.

ringlet—A very narrow ring.

ring system—A set of rings around a giant planet, made up of fine rocky and icy particles.

rotation—The spin of a body around its own axis.

shepherd moon—A tiny moon located near a planet's rings that may help keep the ring particles in place through the force of gravity.

space probe—An unmanned spacecraft, carrying scientific instruments, used to explore another planet or moon.

Chapter 1. The Jewel of the Solar System
1. E.C. Krupp, *Echoes of the Ancient Skies: The Astronomy of Lost Civilizations* (New York: Harper & Row Publishers, 1983), p. 70.

2. Ibid., p. 81.

3. William Sheehan, *Worlds in the Sky* (Tucson: The University of Arizona Press, 1992), p. 132.

4. James Reston, Jr., *Galileo* (New York: Harper Collins Publishers, 1994), p. 105.

5. Sheehan, p. 133.

Chapter 2. The Ringed Planet
1. Thomas R. Watters, *Planets: A Smithsonian Guide* (New York: Macmillan, 1995), p. 146.

2. Giovanni Caprara, *The Solar System* (Buffalo: Firefly Books, Inc., 2002), p. 159.

Chapter 3. Saturn's Mysterious Rings
1. Giovanni Caprara, *The Solar System* (Buffalo: Firefly Books, Inc., 2002), p. 163.

2. Thomas R. Watters, *Planets: A Smithsonian Guide* (New York: Macmillan, 1995), p. 149.

3. Ibid., p. 151.

Chapter 4. The Moons of Saturn
1. Thomas R. Watters, *Planets: A Smithsonian Guide* (New York: Macmillan, 1995), p. 154.

2. Carl Sagan, *Cosmos* (New York: Random House, 1980), p. 162.

Chapter 5. The Exploration of Saturn
1. J. Kelly Beatty, Carolyn Collins Petersen, and Andrew Chaikin, *The New Solar System* (Cambridge, Mass.: Cambridge University Press, 1999), p. 237.

2. Ibid., p. 278.

3. Ibid., p. 279.

4. *The New York Times,* John Noble Wilford, "European Craft on Saturn Moon Finds Tantalizing Signs of Liquid," January 15, 2005, <http://www.nytimes.com/2005/01/15/international/europe/15titan.html?oref=login> (February 28, 2005).

5. European Space Agency News, "Seeing, Touching and Smelling the Extraordinarily Earth-like World of Titan," January 21, 2005, <http://www.esa.int/esaCP/SEMHB881Y3E_index_0.html> (February 28, 2005).

6. Ibid.

Asimov, Isaac, with revisions and updating by Richard Hantula. *Saturn*. Milwaukee: Gareth Stevens, Inc., 2003.

Bortolotti, Dan. *Exploring Saturn*. Toronto: Firefly Books, 2003.

Cole, Michael D. *Saturn—The Sixth Planet*. Berkeley Heights, N.J.: Enslow Publishers, Inc., 2002.

Harland, David M. *Mission to Saturn: Cassini and the Huygens Probe*. New York: Springer, 2002.

Kerrod, Robin. *Saturn*. Minneapolis: Lerner Publications, 2000.

Ridpath, Ian. *Facts on File Stars and Planets Atlas*. New York: Facts on File, 2001.

Spangenburg, Ray, and Kit Moser. *A Look at Moons*. New York: Franklin Watts, 2000.

Stone, Tanya Lee. *Saturn*. Tarrytown, N.Y.: Benchmark Books, 2002.

Vogt, Gregory. *Jupiter, Saturn, Uranus, and Neptune*. Austin, Tex.: Steadwell Books, 2001.

Whitehouse, Patricia. *The Planets*. Chicago: Heinemann Library, 2005.

Wolverton, Mark. *The Depths of Space: The Story of the Pioneer Planetary Probes*. Washington, D.C.: Joseph Henry Press, 2004.